DAREDEVIL
SPORTS

MMA

By Peter Castellano

HOT TOPICS

Please visit our website, www.garethstevens.com. For a free color catalog of all our high-quality books, call toll free 1-800-542-2595 or fax 1-877-542-2596.

Castellano, Peter.
MMA / by Peter Castellano.
p. cm. — (Daredevil sports)
Includes index.
ISBN 978-1-4824-2981-7 (pbk.)
ISBN 978-1-4824-2980-0 (6 pack)
ISBN 978-1-4824-2982-4 (library binding)
1. Mixed martial arts — Juvenile literature. I. Title.
GV1102.7 C37 2016
796.815—d23

First Edition

Published in 2016 by
Gareth Stevens Publishing
111 East 14th Street, Suite 349
New York, NY 10003

Designer: Nicholas Domiano
Editor: Kristen Rajczak

Photo credits: Cover (background front), p. 1 Chris Hyde/Getty Images Sport/ Getty Images; cover (background back) nobeastsofierce/Shutterstock.com; p. 5 Suhaimi Abdullah/Getty Images Sport/Getty Images; pp. 7, 21 Alex Trautwig/Getty Images Sport/Getty Images; p. 8 Mark Kolbe/Getty Images Sport/Getty Images; p. 9 Jonathan Ferry/Getty Images Sport/Getty Images; p. 11 Michael Ochs Archives/Moviepix/ Getty Images; p. 12 Sankei Archive/Sankei/Getty Images; p. 13 Terry O'Neill/ Getty Images; p. 15 Holly Stein/Getty Images Sport/Getty Images; p. 16 Tang Chhin Sothy/Getty Images; pp. 17, 23, 29 Victor Fraile/Getty Images Sport/Getty Images; pp. 19, 24 Christian Petersen/Getty Images Sport/Getty Images; p. 25 Diamond Images/Getty Images; p. 27 Xaume Olleros/Getty Images Sport/Getty Images.

Printed in the United States of America

CPSIA compliance information: Batch # **CS15GS**: For further information contact Gareth Stevens, New York, New York at 1-800-542-2595.

CONTENTS

What Is MMA?   4

MMA History   10

Inside the Cage   16

Knock 'Em Down!   22

Many Rules   24

Staying Safe in MMA   30

For More Information   31

Glossary   32

Index   32

WHAT IS MMA?

Two fighters face each other in an MMA **bout**, daring one another to throw a punch. Finally, one does. His **opponent** ducks and tries a kick. Each fighter grabs the other around the neck, and one is pushed to the ground. The crowd around them roars.

RISK-FACTOR

All MMA fighting and training should be done with the help of a good coach. It's unsafe to try MMA moves on your own.

"MMA" stands for "mixed martial arts." It's a sport that mixes many styles of martial arts from around the world. MMA fighters have training in several different **disciplines**. However, since they all come from different martial arts backgrounds, fighters each have their own **style**.

RISK FACTOR

Both men and women **compete** in MMA, though not against each other.

MMA fighters use moves that come from boxing, wrestling, karate, tae kwon do, and Brazilian jujitsu, among other martial arts disciplines. They learn to use parts of each when preparing to fight in MMA. Training in freestyle wrestling, for example, helps a fighter learn to take down opponents quickly.

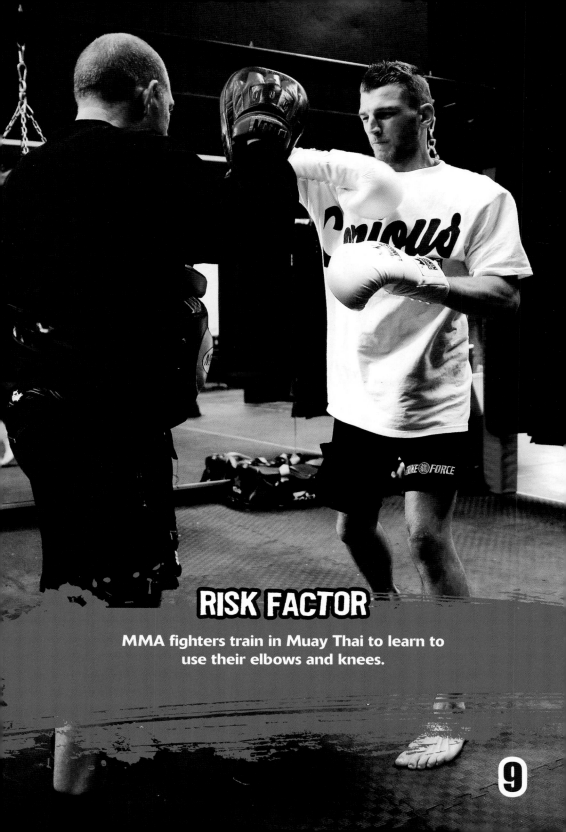

RISK FACTOR

MMA fighters train in Muay Thai to learn to
use their elbows and knees.

MMA HISTORY

Different fighting disciplines faced off as early as the late 1800s. Then, Asian martial artists took on European fighters in England. In 1887, a boxing champion fought a wrestler named William Muldoon. Muldoon took him down in minutes.

RISK FACTOR

Actor Bruce Lee created jeet kune do in 1967. Some call him the first modern mixed martial artist.

In 1976, American boxer Muhammad Ali fought Japanese martial artist Antonio Inoki. After 15 rounds, it ended in a draw, or tie. Many people believe the outcome was faked, but because Ali was so famous, the fight got many people interested in two disciplines competing.

RISK FACTOR

Ali made $6 million to fight Inoki. Inoki made $2 million.

13

In 1993, a group of martial artists and fighters wanted to know which discipline was the best. They planned an event putting the best in each against one another to find out. This was the first Ultimate Fighting Championship (UFC) event.

RISK FACTOR

The UFC is the best-known MMA organization. Strikeforce and World Extreme Cagefighting were two others, but they were both bought by the company that owns the UFC.

INSIDE THE CAGE

Since 1993, MMA has become very popular. MMA bouts take place on a raised **canvas** fighting surface, surrounded by a cage. The cage keeps the fighters safe. It stops them from falling to the floor or into the crowd.

RISK FACTOR

In the UFC, the fighting area is called the "octagon" because it has eight sides.

17

Crowds get their money's worth at MMA events! During an MMA competition, there are several bouts lasting three rounds each. Fighters hit each other with punches, elbows, and knees. They throw one another into the cage or to the ground.

RISK FACTOR

Rounds are 5 minutes long. Championship bouts have five rounds of 5 minutes each.

Three judges sit on different sides of the cage during a bout. They watch the fighters carefully and give each one a score to decide who wins the round. An MMA fight can end with the judges choosing the winner based on the points fighters earned.

RISK FACTOR

When the judges' points establish a winner, it's called winning by "decision."

21

KNOCK 'EM DOWN!

Fights can also end in a knockout, or when one fighter blacks out during a fight. In a technical knockout (TKO), a **referee** or doctor announces a winner when one fighter stops fighting back. A doctor announces a TKO when continuing the fight seems unsafe for one of the fighters.

RISK FACTOR

A fight can end by "submission," when one fighter has trapped their opponent in a certain hold. The trapped fighter shows they've given up by saying so or by tapping the mat or the other fighter.

23

MANY RULES

When the UFC started, MMA had few rules. Today, most MMA competitions use a set of rules called the Unified Rules of Mixed Marital Arts, but some rules can be different from event to event. They also have to follow the laws of the state they're in.

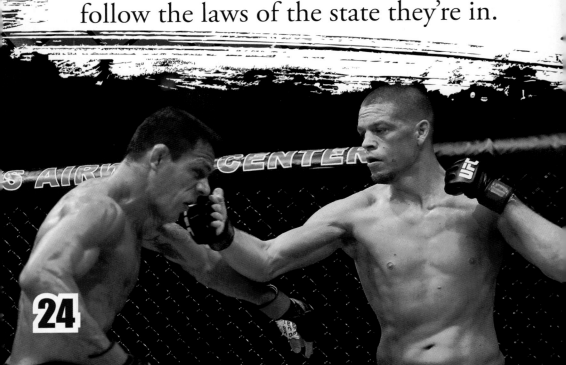

RISK FACTOR

The Unified Rules of Mixed Martial Arts state the size of the cage, give directions about judging, and even tell fighters how to wrap their hands.

All fighters must be weighed to make sure they're fighting someone close to their weight. The weight classes in MMA include featherweight, lightweight, heavyweight, and more. Fighters have to weigh in before each bout they compete in.

RISK FACTOR

Weight classes make sports like MMA fairer.

MMA fighters lose points for breaking rules. There's no biting, hair pulling, grabbing of the throat, or kneeing the head of an opponent on the ground. MMA can be a dangerous sport. Fighters may kick, throw, and punch their opponents—but they don't want to injure them too much.

RISK FACTOR

Fighters can be disqualified, or taken out of the bout, for breaking too many rules.

STAYING SAFE IN MMA

MMA FIGHTERS SHOULD:

- follow the rules when fighting an opponent.

- never compete injured.

- not compete too often in order to allow their body to recover between bouts.

- train to be as fit as they can. It will help them hold up during bouts better and recover more easily.

- know how to keep themselves safe when facing an opponent.

FOR MORE INFORMATION

BOOKS

Polydoros, Lori. *MMA Greats*. North Mankato, MN: Capstone Press, 2012.

Whiting, Jim. *A New Generation of Warriors: The History of Mixed Martial Arts*. Mankato, MN: Capstone Press, 2010.

WEBSITES

Martial Arts Styles

www.ufc.com/discover/fighter/martialArtsStyles/
Find out more about the blend of fighting styles used in MMA.

MMA Fighting

mmafighting.com
Read about the latest events and some of the best fighters competing today.

GLOSSARY

bout: an athletic match

canvas: a strong cloth

compete: to try to win in a contest

discipline: a kind of training

opponent: the person or team you must beat to win a game

referee: an official who makes sure players follow the rules

style: a certain way of doing something

INDEX

Ali, Muhammad 12, 13

bout 4, 16, 18, 20, 26, 29, 30

boxing 8, 10

cage 16, 18, 20, 25

Inoki, Antonio 12, 13

jeet kune do 10

judges 20

jujitsu 8

karate 8

knockout 22

Lee, Bruce 10

Muay Thai 9

octagon 17

rules 24, 25, 28, 29, 30

submission 23

tae kwon do 8

TKO 22

UFC 14, 15, 17, 24

weight classes 26, 27

wrestling 8, 10